10667075

VERMEER

T&J

This edition published 2009

Published by
TAJ BOOKS INTERNATIONAL LLP
27 Ferndown Gardens
Cobham
Surrey
KT11 2BH
UK
www.tajbooks.com

Design and layout Copyright © TAJ Books International LLP

All notations of errors or omissions (author inquiries, permissions) concerning the content of this book should be addressed to info@tajbooks.com.

ISBN: 978-1-84406-124-2

VERMEER

BY SANDRA FORTY

JOHANNES VERMEER 1632 -75

INTRODUCTION

The wonderful, serene paintings of Jan Vermeer—although sadly few in number—show a world of Dutch order and domestic calm. His work illuminates the quiet life of ordinary Dutch men and, particularly, women going about their lives: cleaning, chatting, cooking, drinking, playing music, and quietly contemplating life. Their existence is shown as measured and predictable, comfortable but not glamorous, unhurried and orderly with nothing out of place.

Vermeer painted the prosperous burghers of Delft, who wanted visible proof of their position in life through the medium of oil and canvas—as so many wealthy patrons of art have done and continue to do. But instead of heroic poses or classical settings, Vermeer shows them in their own homes providing us with a wonderful view into their lives and way of life. This was the ideal the wealthy merchants aspired to: diligent wife, dutiful children, the restrained dignity of domestic decoration. Indeed, all the historical evidence points to their houses being as tidy and orderly as Vermeer shows. These calm and secure lives are in contrast to the outside world of the time. The Low Countries was in political turmoil with the Dutch Republic struggling to establish economic and social independence from a circle of surrounding enemies—most notably Spain, France, and England, the latter being the Dutch Republic's main sea-trading rival against whom the Dutch would fight a string of naval wars in the later seventeenth century

HISTORICAL BACKGROUND

To understand the period in which Vermeer lived and painted it is necessary to go back into the sixteenth century and a period of great religious strife in Europe following the Protestant Reformation started by *Martin Luther* (1483–1546). Broadly, the southern provinces of the Low Countries were Roman Catholic and the northern provinces Protestant, some of them dominated by the extremist Calvinists who abhorred anything but work, worship, and Christian ethics. During the sixteenth century all these provinces were called the "Spanish Netherlands" and were ruled by the Spanish Hapsburg Empire that dominated Western Europe. Spanish Catholic rule was deeply resented by the predominantly Protestant Dutch, and so the Netherlands became the "cockpit of Europe" as the inhabitants tried to throw off the Spanish yoke. With the southern provinces helped by French monarchs, who coveted their lands, and the northern assisted by their Protestant neighbors—primarily the north German states and England—the bloody, bitter revolt in the Netherlands would inspire generations of Dutch painters such as the two *Pieter Breughels* (the Older c.1520–1569, the Younger c.1564–1638).

To strengthen their hand the seven northern states banded together by the *Union of Utrecht* (1579) under the leadership of the house of Orange-Nassau, then ruled by *William the Silent* (1533–1584). After the death of *King Philip II of Spain* in 1598, the revolt continued until his successor, *Philip III*, agreed to a twelve-year truce in 1609. In effect this granted independence to the northern–the "United Provinces"–and concluded eighty years of struggle. At long last the United Provinces were recognized as independent and their merchants were permitted to trade in the east and west Indies.

The Dutch could now start a new era as an important power in Europe, something that would bring both good and bad things to the country. On the one hand it would push the United Provinces into a love/hate relationship with their erstwhile allies England. There would be three wars between the two countries in 1652–54, 1665–67, and 1672–74, but in 1688 the Protestants of England would offer the throne to *William of Orange*, who would rule that country in partnership with his wife, Mary, between 1688 and 1702. On the other hand, the hard-working burghers of the United Provinces saw trade– including the start of the infamous slave trade that would become so important in the eighteenth century–bringing unprecedented wealth into the country. This, in turn, led to a blossoming of the arts.

Dutch society was officially tolerant of religious conscience: both Catholics and Protestants lived side by side, mostly without rancor. But the Protestant work ethic already ran far and deep within Dutchmen and, encouraged by their government, they were anxious to expand their economic boundaries across the trading world. Consequently Dutch bankers and merchants were left free by their government to do much as they wished to attract foreign firms and money into the Dutch economy. The Dutch proved to possess a natural talent for ruthless competition which provided for a self-confident society fueled by commercial success. As part of this endeavor, Amsterdam established itself as the principal money market of Europe. The Netherlands rapidly became a very prosperous area and one of the few not to regularly suffer from famine.

Calvinism, with its teaching and encouragement of thrift and commerce, lay at the root of Dutch mercantile success. The Dutch economic foundation was the fishing industry, which in one way or another employed one fifth of the Dutch population. This, in turn, stimulated shipbuilding and associated trades and very soon Dutch ships controlled the coastal trade around the English Channel, North Sea, and Baltic. Dutch wealth depended less on exports than on the transport of goods between other countries and Dutch ships dominated in particular the Baltic trade and monopolized trade between Russia and western Europe. Following on from this success, the founding of the Dutch East and West India companies brought immense riches to the Netherlands, as well as exotic goods such as spices and silks. All trade was guaranteed by Dutch maritime power and such prosperity suffered badly in times of conflict.

The wealth that came from Dutch competition on the world mercantile trading routes was brought back home and profits were reinvested in trading companies, the banks, and land reclamation schemes rather than in industry. Successful trade produced a wealthy and educated merchant class that was anxious to impress the world with its style and importance. Such people became the patrons of the thriving Dutch artistic community as these prosperous middle class burghers sought works of art to fill their homes. The number of artists expanded as demand increased and the Dutch economic prosperity of the seventeenth century fueled the heyday of Dutch painting.

This patronage of Dutch painting by wealthy merchants was quite different to that in many other countries. As a republic in a time of monarchies, the Dutch had important political families—such as the house of Nassau-Orange, that would provide the monarch for England in 1688—but unlike other countries where the patrons were the church, royalty, and wealthy nobility who demanded opulent and ostentatious works of art, the Dutch patrons were hard working and prosperous merchants, often Calvinists. Calvinism was an austere form of Protestantism whose adherents believed in predestination and whose civic life was closely controlled by the church.

In spite of the severity of Calvinism, the arts thrived although, interestingly, there were few sculptors: the teachings of Calvin vilified the graven image as popish. So at a time when the great catholic sculptors such as Bernini flourished, in the Protestant north they were few and far between. The wealthy merchants of Amsterdam did not flaunt their wealth as the nobility of other countries but instead commissioned solid, dignified, domestic art. Many such merchants and farmers became the patrons of artists as a popular expression of achievement even for a relatively ordinary Dutch family. They wanted realistic portrayals of everyday life—not religious or allegorical essays in paint and imagination.

VERMEER'S CONTEMPORARIES

This then is the political background of the period in which Vermeer painted. What of his contemporaries? Vermeer was only one of many artists working in the Netherlands in the seventeenth century; out of an average population of some 2,500,000, there are 3,000 known seventeenth century Dutch artists. The lesser contemporaries of Vermeer include, to mention just a few:

- *Hendrick Avercamp* (1585–1634), similar to Brueghel, with densely populated paintings of peasants going about their business
- *Ambrosius Bosschaert* (1573–1621), whose flower paintings set standards that took many years to surpass
- *Albert Cuyp* (1620–91), who painted bucolic landscapes of summer
- *Pieter Claesz* (c.1597–1660), renowned for his perfect still lives
- *Jan van Goyen* (1596–1656), a painter of landscapes and seascapes much sought-after today, particularly those of rivers, mud flats, estuaries, and huge skies
- *Meyndert Hobbema* (1638–1709), best known for his Avenue at Middelharnis and his landscapes and skies

- *Pieter de Hoogh* (1629–83), whose detailed domestic interiors anticipate Vermeer's work
- *Paulus Potter* (1625–54), a promising animal painter who died young.
- *Jacob van Ruisdael* (c.1600–70), perhaps the most famous painter of somber and dramatic Dutch lowland landscapes
- *Pieter Saenredam* (1597–1665), with his meticulously precise church interiors
- *Willem van de Velde* (1633–1707), the most famous of the many brilliant Dutch painters of ships and the sea.

Head and shoulders above these Dutch artists, however, were two men—*Frans Hals* (c.1580–1666) and *Rembrandt* (1606–69). They may not have been regarded so by their contemporaries, but history has placed these two and Vermeer at the very pinnacle of the art world as three of the world's greatest painters. Hals, from Antwerp, was a portrait painter—everyone remembers The Laughing Cavalier—who was never short of commissions and was as highly regarded in his time as Rembrandt. As with so many great artists, however, Hals was increasingly debt-ridden and died in relative poverty in Haarlem where he had lived most of his life and whose patronage included a small stipend in his later years.

The most successful Dutch painter of the period—some would say ever—was Rembrandt Harmensz. van Rijn, better known simply as Rembrandt. Born in Leiden but most closely associated with Amsterdam, the hugely prosperous capital of the Netherlands, Rembrandt was successful during his lifetime and in the centuries since his oeuvre has become more and more popular—for the remarkable variety of his subject matter, the many portraits of his wife Saskia, the warts-and-all self-portraits, and the brilliance of his understanding of light and shade. His greatest paintings outside his wonderful self-portraits is probably The Night Watch.

Johannes Vermeer, Portrait of the artist

VERMEER'S LIFE AND WORKS

The facts about the life of Johannes Vermeer are tantalizingly few and far between. Although he is now regarded as one of the greatest of Dutch artists, during his lifetime he was—as discussed above—just one of many working in the Dutch Republic.

Vermeer was born, lived, worked, and died in the fine medieval town of Delft, lying a few miles inland from the North Sea coast and one of the most important cities in the Netherlands. Delft, in the province of Holland, had a population in the seventeenth century of about 20,000 souls. A few of these were nobles, but there was as well a sizeable class of wealthy merchants and townsmen who outnumbered countrymen two to one. Delft had became rich through pottery: Delft tiles in particular were in demand across the Continent. The town was also well known for its thriving tapestry-weaving industry and its breweries.

Delft was governed by a traditionally minded town council that was drawn from a small class of prosperous burghers. These men—who would be Vermeer's patrons and subjects—ran the town and local government: in 1445 a charter had granted the "wise and rich" citizens to choose forty of the "the wisest and richest, most honorable, notable, and peaceful" for the duke to select the regents of the town.

Vermeer was born in 1632 to *Digna Balthasars* and *Reynier Jansz. Vos.* The records show that he was baptized into the Dutch Reformed

Church at the Neuwe Kerk in Delft on October 31, 1632, so he was probably born a few days earlier. His father, also a native of Delft, was at the time working in the silk trade as a weaver producing "caffa"—a fine satin fabric—but in 1641 he was sufficiently wealthy enough to buy the "Mechelen" inn situated in the Grote Markt area of Delft. However, like many of his Dutch contemporaries he persued a sideline, his was working as an art dealer and valuer.

Even less is known about Vermeer's education and early training, but it is known that he became an apprentice painter in Delft in about 1647—long before the Delft school of painting was regarded as having any importance. He would have served a standard artist's apprenticeship of about six years' duration. He probably studied under Hendrick van der Burgh but no evidence has been found to confirm this. Alternatively, his teacher may have been *Leonaert Bramer* (1596–1674), a very well-regarded painter of historic and religious scenes. Vermeer's early work was, however, influenced by *Carel Fabritius* (1622–54), a pupil of Rembrandt. Fabritius came to Delft in 1651, some years after the start of Vermeer's apprenticeship, and may well have become one of the greatest Dutch painters. Tragically he was killed at the age of 32 when a powder magazine exploded, wrecking a large portion of Delft and causing considerable loss of life.

Vermeer's work also seems to have been influenced by the Utrecht followers of Caravaggio—such as Hendrick Terbrugghen—who emulated the Italian's dramatic use of light and shade, chiaroscuro, to model his figures. Dutch painters of this period tended to remain and work in their own towns without reference to or interaction with painters working in others. Each town developed its own style, and within each town there was great diversity as the many artists struggled and competed to make a living. However, there was some movement between the locations and it is possible that Vermeer went to Utrecht or even Amsterdam to study: we cannot be sure because there are no records of him for this period. There is also an argument for him to have traveled to Italy to study the great masters there, but again there is no hard evidence of this.

The chief centers for artists in the Dutch Republic were Amsterdam (easily the biggest and most lucrative area for an artist to work, but also the most competitive), Utrecht, Leiden, Haarlem, and Delft. Several thousand painters were working at the same time as Vermeer, many in Delft itself, and many were competing for the same commissions as him. Given these circumstances it is not surprising that many artists highly regarded today were overlooked by patrons within their own lifetimes and that artists came into and fell out of favor—and the wherewithal to live well in society.

Vermeer was registered as a master painter of the Delft painters' Guild of St Luke on December 29, 1653. That same year, on April 20, he married Catharina Bolnes, a girl from a wealthy Catholic family, against the express wishes of her mother who wanted Vermeer to convert to Catholicism before the marriage. His mother-in-law to be, Maria Thins, had distinct Jesuit leanings and objected to the union so much that on April 5 she went before a notary to swear a statement conveying her misgivings. Luckily for the young couple, however, she also agreed not to stop her daughter marrying where her heart lay. This statement was witnessed by the prominent Delft painter Leonaert Bramer. Fortunately for marital harmony, there was obviously a reconciliation with mother-in-law, as by 1660 Johannes, Catharina, and Maria Thins were all living together in her house on the Oude Langendijck in the "Papists' Corner" of Delft. Thins is also known to have helped the couple financially from time to time. It is quite possible that Vermeer had converted to Catholicism to allay her fears. One thing is certain: his marriage produced many children—eleven are known—so his household must have been a lot more lively than some of his paintings intimate.

In his early work Vermeer had yet to develop his style and, in common with many young artists of the time, he painted large-scale religious and genre paintings such as the *Procuress* (1656). He used an impasto technique of laying on the paint quite thickly; but as he matured as a painter his painting grew more refined to produce a smoother surface with no trace of brushstrokes to distract attention from his subject. His aim was to convey a huge variety of texture in textiles and materials with the play of light and shadow across the surface. In later years his technique refined further to become more clearly defined and harder with less room for suggestion.

The Delft school of painting took off in the 1650s as other painters such as *Jan Steen*, *Pieter de Hoogh* (both arrived in Delft in 1654), *Paulus Potter*, and *Fabritius* moved to the city. But of the Delft school Vermeer was the most prominent if not the most successful. The Procuress dates from this period. By about 1660 Vermeer had developed his characteristic style of immaculately observed, highly detailed paintings, and in the years following produced his most definitive works. By this time his palette had changed to become altogether lighter and his colors cooler—with blues, yellows, and sometimes red dominant in his compositions, singling out a particular aspect of each painting. Shadows become less intrusive and blend away into the background. Light was important, the vast Dutch skies give a particular light that gives a translucent quality to all it touches. Vermeer emphasized this quality by painting in such a way as to hide his brushstrokes, almost to provide a photographic quality to his work. Such meticulous technique was hugely time-consuming and probably accounts for the very small number of paintings he is known to have completed—although the lack of a large studio with many willing hands to assist also contributed to this.

His reputation among Delft artists was established by this time—so much so that in 1662–63 and then again in 1669–70 he was appointed to the prestigious position of headman of the governing body of the Delft painters' guild. Yet he still had difficulty selling his work; his fellow Delft painters certainly admired him but, unlike so many of his contemporaries, his work was not esteemed by the buying public and none of his paintings seem to have sold in the saleroom for as much money as that reached by the work of other, lesser, artists. Perhaps his narrow range of subject matter did not appeal sufficiently; perhaps the time he took over even the smallest of paintings; perhaps it was just the sheer weight of competition: whatever the reason, Johannes Vermeer was one of the many great painters whose works have made only later owners rich.

The Delft School of painters specialized in the study of perspective, particularly in relation to buildings and especially of interiors. Vermeer and his fellow artists are known to have used a camera obscura to accurately render a composition. Just how much Vermeer relied on a camera obscura is a heavily debated subject. The camera obscura was simply a darkened box with an aperture for light to enter and project the image of external objects via a focusing tube and convex lens onto a surface such as a wall or a canvas. It helps an artist to get proportion and perspective correct.

The appearance of such mechanical aids typified the period. The seventeenth century was an age of great advances in science with new discoveries exciting even the general public. The improvement in lenses allowed a closer observation of everyday objects, and day-to-day subjects gained a greater interest, particularly to a constituency whose living relied on observation. One of Delft's most renowned citizens of the period was *Antony van Leeuwenhoek* (1632–1723). Almost certainly acquainted with Vermeer, Leeuwenhoek was a local draper and amateur naturalist who had become interested in microscopes. The instruments available at the time could only magnify around 60 to 80 times. Leeuwenhoek painstakingly ground his own lens which was almost spherical. When mounted between two plates it achieved magnifications of up to 300 times, opening up an entirely new world of microbiology. He would go on to discover *bacteria in the tartar of teeth* (1676), the *existence of blood corpuscles* (1674), and the *structure of nerves* (1717)

On his father's death in 1655 Vermeer took over the "Mechelen" inn and continued to run his father's art-dealing shop for the rest of his life. As an example of the sort of work he undertook, in 1672 he was approached to authenticate a collection of Italian paintings in The Hague. Having two or more professions was not unusual at the time: painting alone was often not sufficient to earn a living. Indeed, even Rembrandt ran a business, and Vermeer's fellow Delft painter Jan Steen ran a brewery in the city in the 1650s.

As far as we can tell today, Vermeer worked exclusively in oils. His subject was the minutiae of the everyday world around him, especially interiors. His lack of prosperity was no doubt a reflection of his very slow and meticulous method of painting. At the time his work was so individual and different that patrons were hard to acquire, and seem to have been put off by his unconventionality. His main contemporary collector appears to have been a Delft bookseller and dealer, Jacob Dissius, who is known to have owned around twenty of Vermeer's paintings. He inherited at least some Vermeers and may have bought a few himself, but how much he paid for them and whether he bought them directly from Vermeer is not known. (The Dissius collection was sold in its entirety in Amsterdam after his death in 1696.) It is known that Vermeer had a few regular clients including Pieter Claesz. van Ruijven, an important townsman of Delft, but for Vermeer wealthy clients were few and far between.

Vermeer seems to have became famous locally in Delft but his influence does not seem to have traveled far in his lifetime. He seems rarely to have sold a painting, although when he did it apparently paid well: one is known to have sold for 600 guilders, although fashionable Amsterdam painters could command much higher prices for their work. The money he received for his work did not last for long and he seems to have been often in debt. He probably lived comfortably until the art market collapsed in 1672 when France invaded the Netherlands and panic hit the population. Certainly foreign collectors visited his studio when they visited Delft and one, *Balthasar de Monconys*, a Frenchman who inspected his work in 1663, thought that his prices were too high. Vermeer's only other known admirer was the local baker, but his three paintings may well have been payment in lieu of money for the Vermeer family's bread bills—the artist's time-honored answer to financial problems.

Otherwise Vermeer dealt in works of art and was regarded as a skilled valuer, but he lived from hand to mouth much of the time.

The mid-seventeenth century saw politics once more come to the fore with war against England and problems with France. Funding for the arts and culture lessened and artists like Vermeer, already living a financially precarious existence, fell on very hard times. The ebb and flow of politics are a long way from art, but war meant the diversion of money into other areas. The respite from war afforded by the truce with Spain was threatened by the danger of a territorially aggressive France. The French king—Le Roi Soleil himself, Louis XIV (1638–1715) had acceded to the throne at age five in 1643. In 1651, his minority over, he took command of his nation determined to aggrandize himself and France. During his minority France had been governed by his mother and Cardinal Jules Mazarin, who had done much to prepare the ground for him. Indeed, by 1648 Spain had lost so much ground politically and economically that she purchased Dutch neutrality against France. At the same time, the Dutch embarked on a bitter war with kingless England over trade in 1651. Oliver Cromwell's Commonwealth proved too strong for the Dutch and after a corrosive war which did much to damage the Dutch trade, the Treaty of Westminster brought peace in 1654.

In 1665 the war flared up again and again trading routes and rights were in dispute. Peace came more swiftly this time—by the treaty of Breda in 1667—following a brilliant naval campaign by Michiel de

Ruyter that included a foray into the River Medway itself where he took the English fleet's flagship Royal Charles. The peace with the English was a brief respite, for almost immediately that same year the Netherlands found themselves at war with France when Louis XIV invaded Brabant. In 1672 the French went further and invaded the United Provinces themselves; this time the dykes were breeched to prevent the French taking Amsterdam thus saving Holland and Zeeland from French control.

Vermeer died in 1675 in Delft at age 43. He was so deeply in debt by this time that his estate was declared insolvent. Almost the only thing he could leave his wife were what was left of his paintings, twenty-nine of them, and three by Fabritius, his mentor. Other objects left included the ebony crucifix and gilt leather panel both seen in his *Allegory of Faith* painted c.1671. Leeuwenhoek, who by this time held the biology chair at the university of Leiden, was appointed by the city fathers of Delft as the executor of Vermeer's estate—a tricky business as his many debts left various counterclaims on his legacy. On March 15, 1677, van Leeuwenhoek held a sale of paintings from Vermeer's estate to raise money for his creditors. A few months after Vermeer's death his widow had to apply for a writ of insolvency. She gave the French invasion of the Netherlands as the reason for lack of demand for her husband's work and his inability to make a living from painting.

VERMEER'S LEGACY

Vermeer was lucky to be painting at a time of great Dutch expansion and prosperity. The United Provinces was a wealthy country, rich from overseas trade. The Dutch East and West India Companies had brought huge profits and exotic goods into the Netherlands. The center and most prosperous city was Amsterdam, but Delft where Vermeer lived and worked also profited. Although only moderately successful and only known locally, he made a sufficient living in his short lifetime to allow him to complete the small oeuvre we know today. After his death many of his paintings disappeared from the records and were only rediscovered centuries later. Vermeer and his works were forgotten and his paintings lay mostly unregarded in obscure corners, overlooked by their owners and custodians.

Vermeer's obscurity remained for 200 years after his death until he was rediscovered in France by an enthusiastic art critic in the nineteenth century. In 1866 the French critic and scholar *Étienne Thoré* (1807–69) who used the nom de plume William Bürger, published three articles in the Gazette des Beaux-Arts about Vermeer's work, in the process drawing it to the attention of the Impressionist painters. In fact so great was Thoré's admiration of Jan Vermeer that he made it his personal quest to discover the lost masterpieces and he traveled the length and breadth of Europe searching for Vermeer's. There were disappointingly few to be found, perhaps because of the long duration of his obscurity, under

40 pictures are attributed to Vermeer altogether and it is perfectly possible given his financial insecurity, meticulously slow technique, and sadly early death, that he did not paint many more.

Today, however, our view of Vermeers precise, simple work is different. His absolute mastery of technique—look at the wonderful detail in the maps behind the figure in Woman in blue reading a letter or An Allegory of Painting—his understated use of color, the intimacy of his subject matter: all these factors make him valued today. Indeed his position in the artistic pantheon places him in the highest rank as one of the most outstanding artists ever. Vermeer shows us everyday life without embroidery but with considerable love, understanding, and intense attention to detail.

Vermeer specialized in the domestic life of the prosperous burgher who wanted his goods and chattels—and often his wife—immortalized in paint. His gift was to quietly illuminate the burghers sources of pride in prudence, order, and domestic stability. The homes that Vermeer depicted were so perfect that it is hard to believe that people lived in them, they are presentation rooms of perfection, almost as if they are still lives, but they are exactly the way people at that time, the seventeenth century, and in that place, Delft, lived. Although people sparsely populate his paintings their stillness has a unique quality of permanence, the impression they leave is of substance and personality, the more you look at them the more there is to be seen hidden in the detail. This intense scrutiny is given immense beauty through Vermeer's treatment of light which floods into his interiors picking out the subdued quality of the subjects. He is truly an artist of exceptional ability and unique comment.

SAINT PRAXEDIS

1655; 40in x 32½in (101.6cm x 82.6cm); oil on canvas.
Barbara Piasecka Johnson Collection Foundation, Princeton, New Jersey

Dated to 1655, two years after he was registered as a master painter, this painting has only recently been positively attributed to Vermeer. It is not typical of the work generally associated with the artist but harkens back Renaissance Italy. It was part of an artist's apprenticeship to copy the works of the great masters in order to learn the craft and in this painting the young Vermeer freely copied a painting by Felice Ficherelli, a Florentine. Saint Praxedis is consequently used as evidence that Vermeer traveled to Italy to study the works of the great Italian masters. He certainly had a scholarly knowledge of Italian painting but there is no direct evidence of a journey there.

What is slightly surprising at first glance is the subject matter of the painting-a Catholic saint-for a young Dutch artist of the time. St Praxedis was cannonized for working with the bodies of dead martyrs and Vermeer pictures her washing the blood from the body of a headless corpse, although the corpse is left discreetly in the background. The crucifix in her hand symbolizes the mingling of Christ's blood with that of his new martyr. At right in the far background is her sister, St Pudentia, entering an Italianate building.

It is possible, after his marriage in 1653 to Catholic Catharina Bolnes, that the painting was executed to celebrate his own conversion. Alternatively, it may have been commissioned by local Jesuits, friends of Vermeer's mother-in-law, who was a devout Catholic. The style may not be the same as his later, better known, work but the delicacy with which he paints St Praxedis's face shows the hand of a true artist.

Plate 1

CHRIST IN THE HOUSE OF MARY AND MARTHA

c.1655; 63in x 55¾in (160cm x 142cm); oil on canvas.
National Gallery of Scotland, Edinburgh

One of Vermeer's earliest paintings, this is only his second surviving religious work. He tackled his third when he was forty, but his fourth, *Three Marys at the Tomb of Christ*, is known of but no longer exists. Unusually for Vermeer *Christ in the House of Mary and Martha* is very dark in composition and completely different from his later light-filled works. The picture was possibly painted to humor his devout mother-in-law, Maria Thins, a woman he had to appease for the sake of domestic happiness, or it could have been painted directly as a commission for one of the burghers of Delft. The figures form a triangular relationship, with Christ looking at Martha but pointing to Mary who is doing all the work while Martha chats.

Plate 2

DIANA WITH HER COMPANIONS

c.1655-1656; 38¾in x 41½in (98.5cm x 105cm); oil on canvas.
Mauritshuis, The Hague

This early work is the only mythological Vermeer painting to have survived- one named *Jupiter*, *Venus* and *Mercury* no longer exists. Here the young Vermeer (he was 22) has adapted Rembrandt's *Bathsheba* (1654) for Diana's pose and takes his theme from Ovid's *Metamorphoses*. This is a popular theme for artists but unlike almost all the others who tackled this subject Vermeer keeps his Diana clothed. Diana is the Roman goddess of hunting and chastity as symbolised by the crescent moon on her head. Two of her bathing companions are washing her feet while the third looks into the distance, perhaps alerted by a noise in the forest. In the myth Diana is disturbed while bathing in the forest by the hunter Actaeon-the grandson of Apollo in Greek mythology. Furious at the intrusion into her privacy she turns him into a stag and sets his own hounds on him. They fail to recognize their master and chase him until they catch him and rip him to pieces.

Vermeer has pictured the scene a few moments before Actaeon's arrival. On the lower left side of the painting the prickly thistle represents Actaeon's impending arrival and the dog indicates his grisly fate.

Plate 3

31

THE PROCURESS

c.1656; 56¼in x 51¼in (143cm x 130cm); oil on canvas.
Staatliche Kunstammlungen, Gemäldegalerie, Dresden

Vermeer's earliest dated painting bears the hallmarks of a young yet proficient painter learning his art. (He only dated two paintings, this and *The Astronomer* of 1668.) The composition is clumsy and uncomfortable, although there is a feeling of assurance in the paint and color tones. Such brothel scenes, or *Bordeeltje*, were popular subjects at the time. It was a way of showing lewd behavior without recourse to the Bible or mythology and also a rejection of the increasingly puritanical teachings of the church. This is a didactic painting with a moral message: the drinking and carousing show that the evils of money and alcohol are seductive. The procuress of the picture's title is the figure in black watching the transaction between the soldier and the woman. The rich tablecloth and silverware gleaming at left show the affluence of the brothel, and the woman's free behavior is clear by the way she is holding out one hand for money while the other clasps a drinking glass. Furthermore, she is unperturbed by the soldier clutching her left breast hardly the reaction of a lady. Her male companions are clearly having a good time and it is possible that the figure at the left of the painting is actually a self-portrait of the young Jan Vermeer.

Plate 4

33

GIRL READING A LETTER AT AN OPEN WINDOW

c.1657; 32¾in x 25½in (83cm x 64.5cm); oil on canvas.
Staatliche Kunstammlungen, Gemäldegalerie, Dresden

This painting is almost monochromatic but for the play of light on the curtains and wall, and the rich dark red of the tablecloth and window drapery-red is the color of love. Framed within the picture by the curtains, rail, and bed the girl is absorbed by the contents of a letter-perhaps from her love. She looks impassive but her letter is crumpled, as if read and reread many times. The open window may signify her secret desire to escape the household and join her lover. She is thrown into silhouette against the pale wall which bringing attention to her serious face and elaborate hairstyle. The carelessly spilled bowl of apples and peaches are a reminder of the perils of the Garden of Eden and the fall of Eve. Here Vermeer treats light and shade more subtly than previously, but his work still has echoes of his earlier adherence to Caravaggio's style. This painting is the first time he uses brilliant dots of impasto paint to produce highlights on the girl's clothes and hair. The light really floods into the picture in a style that would become a Vermeer characteristic.

Plate 5

A GIRL ASLEEP

c.1657; 34½in x 30¼in (87.6cm x 76.5cm); oil on canvas.
The Metropolitan Museum of Art, New York. Bequest of Benjamin Altman, 1913

With this work Vermeer is nearing his mature style. The table laid out in front of the dozing girl is covered with an opulent Turkish rug on which sits an empty wine glass. The fruit looks good enough to eat-Vermeer quietly shows that he could have been a master of still life had he so chosen. To highlight the brass nails on the chairs Vermeer used real gold to make the metal gleam and really stand out from the painting. A Delft jug sits on the table beside the bowl of fresh fruit which symbolize the fall of Eve from the Garden of Eden. The viewer is clearly intended to read a theme of infidelity into the painting. Furthermore, the broken egg was a familiar symbol in seventeenth century Dutch paintings as a synonym for unbridled lust. Modern x-ray examination has shown that Vermeer originally painted a man in the open doorway. Almost forty years after its creation this painting was entitled "A drunken sleeping maid at a table" (*Een dronke slafende Meyd aen een Tafel*) when it was sold in Amsterdam 1696. Forty years later still, in 1737, it was sold again, this time called "A sleeping young woman" (*Een slapent Vrouwtj*).

Plate 6

THE LITTLE STREET

c.1657-1658; 21½in x 17½in (54.3cm x 44cm); oil on canvas.
Rijksmuseum, Amsterdam

It has been suggested that this is either the view of the houses opposite Vermeer's studio window or a composite view of the Voldersgracht in Delft, from the back of Vermeer's tavern, the Mechelen. It is certainly of Delft and is, no doubt, accurate and a loving rendition of the locality. Three of the four figures in the painting are cleaning, the two on their knees are scrubbing the decorative paving and the woman down the alley is doing the washing. The fourth figure is sitting in an open doorway absorbed in her lacemaking. No architectural detail is ignored-even the repaired pointing between the brickwork and the peeling and discolored paint on the shutters and lower portion of the buildings-yet the overwhelming impression is of order and cleanliness. Nothing is out of place, not a scrap of litter or even a hint of mud and certainly no horse droppings, although there would be piles of the latter all over the streets in most other countries.

Plate 7

39

OFFICER AND LAUGHING GIRL

c.1658; 19in x 18¼in (50.5cm x 46cm); oil on canvas.
The Frick Collection, New York

This is considered to be Vermeer's first true masterpiece in his finest mature style. The couple, a girl and a soldier, are clearly enjoying an animated and lively conversation over a glass of something-probably wine. They are both richly dressed in clothes made of costly materials. The soldier and his huge black hat is almost in silhouette against the lighter, brighter, girl and background. Hanging on the wall behind the couple is a large map of Holland. As the Netherlands extended its trading routes around the world, the art of cartography was becoming increasingly popular and wealthy citizens became curious about their surroundings. To own such a map showed the wealth and outward-looking nature of the household. The map is identifiably by Balthasar van Berckenrode and is known to have been dated 1620; the top is facing east and south is at right. This map must have been a favorite of Vermeer's as he included it again in The Love Letter. The rich coloring and play light show that Vermeer is now completely the master of his technique.

Plate 8

THE MILKMAID

c.1658-1660; 18in x 16¼in (45.5cm x 41cm); oil on canvas.
Rijksmuscum, Amsterdam

This is one of Vermeer's few paintings that feature a servant at work as opposed to their masters and mistresses at leisure. The naturalistic pose and skilled use of blues and yellows in particular show that Verrneer was by this time completely confident of his technique. He depicts the servant as a woman of Dutch strength, virtue, and quiet ability. Her mouth is slightly open as if she might be singing to herself as she pours milk into a bowl. All the interest in the composition is In the foreground of the painting: indeed, the arrangement of bread, basket, and cloth is worthy of a still life alone. Dots of impasto paint highlight the table arrangement, and Vermeer uses the optical trick of running a thin white contour down the maid's back for added contrast. On the skirting behind the maid lies a row of typical blue and white Delft tiles depicting traveling artisans. In front of this is a foot warmer-a necessary luxury when the freezing winter winds blow across the Dutch polders. *The Milkmaid* is considered to be Vermeer's earliest surviving genre picture. It was still in his possession when he died and was sold at the auction of his goods in Amsterdam after his death for 175 guilders.

Plate 9

43

THE GLASS OF WINE

c.1658-1660; 25½in x 30¼in (65cm x 77cm); oil on canvas.
Staatliche Museen zu Berlin, Preussischcr Kulturbesitz, Gcmäldegalerie

With this composition Vermeer for the first time stands back from his subject to place them in context within a room. It is one of his truly enigmatic paintings, where the initial impression of the subject is undermined by deeper scrutiny. The lady is in the process of drinking from her glass while the gentleman stands with his hand still holding the Delft jug of wine. His expression is quizzical as if he is waiting for her opinion on the quality of the drink. They are sumptuously, but much less flamboyantly, dressed than the couple in *Officer and Laughing Girl*. To the viewer they are portrayed as an elegant couple but curiously the woman's face is hidden almost entirely-her headdress covers her hair and the wineglass obscures her face. This is a strange device for such an otherwise straightforward painting. Perhaps the drink is the woman's reward for playing music-her instrument lies on the chair in the foreground. Music is often associated with love, and maybe here indicates an intimate association between the couple. The open window throws a little illumination into the room and onto the two figures. The stained glass window bears the arms of Jannetje Vogel (Vermeer's neighbor after she married Moses Nederveen) surrounded by the figure of a woman holding a horse's bridle, a traditional symbol of temperance. (The same window in Vermeer's painting *The Girl with Wineglass*.) In Calvinist teachings women should not be allowed to drink as alcohol was the first step to licentiousness and loose behavior.

Plate 10

THE GIRL WITH WINEGLASS

c.1659-1660; 30¾in x 26½in (78cm x 67cm); oil on canvas.
Herzog Anton Ulrich-Museum, Braunschweig

This composition again steps back from the subjects, although the artist is a little closer than in *The Glass of Wine*. The figures are located in the same room as the previous couple-the floor, stained glass window, and position of the painting on the wall are the same-but this time the couple is joined by a third figure. The latter is clearly bored by the badinage between the man and woman and appears to be dozing beside Vermeer's ubiquitous white Delft jug. The couple themselves are obviously only acquaintances as the girl is turning her head away from the man to conceal her delight at his compliments. He is urging her to try the glass of wine, and judging by the lack of interest from his male companion this is a well-tried technique. The dark and severe portrait on the back wall is probably the master of the house. Is the man a suitor for his daughter or a potential seducer of his wife? This painting belonged to the Duke of Braunschweig (Brunswick) who in 1754 allowed it to be placed on view in the first public gallery in Germany.

Plate 11

VIEW OF DELFT

c.1660-1661; 38¾in x 46¼in (98.5cm x 117.5cm); oil on canvas.
Mauritshuis, The Hague

One of Vermeer's two known outdoor pictures and a homage to his native city of Delft, this is also one of his best known and loved paintings. It was also one of his most highly regarded paintings in his lifetime. A native of Delft would have been able instantly to recognize his home town. In the loving and subtle attention to detail there is every indication that this is a truthful record of Delft, although it is known that Vermeer used artistic license to balance his composition by elongating the edges and compressing the buildings. The clock on the gatehouse shows that the time is seven o'clock, and a bright day of sunshine and showers lies ahead. The town skyline is skilfully shown sandwiched between the huge cloudy sky and the sparkling water. Contemporary maps identify the viewer's position as the upper story of a house across the water from Delft. The skilfully blurred reflections in the shimmering water throw into prominence the buildings and skyline of Vermeer's native city. His use of subtle color modulations and play of light give an intense presence to the painting. Furthermore he mixed a little sand into his paint to evoke the rough surface of the roof tiles. This painting fetched 200 guilders the highest price of all at the Amsterdam auction of the paintings of Delft bookseller Jacob Dissius in 1696.

Plate 12

GIRL INTERRUPTED AT HER MUSIC

c.1660-1661; 15½in x 17½in (39.3cm x 44.4cm); oil on canvas.
The Frick Collection, New York

Another strangely enigmatic painting, all the indications point to love being in the air. First, there is much to do with music-the instrument (*a cittern*) lying on the table with the sheets of music; then there is the large background painting of Cupid holding a bow (with which he shoots his arrows of love) and a playing card that shows love is a matter of chance. But the girl is distracted by the viewer and does not appear interested in the paper that the man is putting in front of her. He appears a lot older than her-perhaps her music teacher-and she seems anxious to hurry off, perhaps to join her lover who has just come into the house. Vermeer also used the painting of Cupid in *A Lady Standing at a Virginal*; it is based on a painting by Cesar van Everdingen. Again, as in so many of Vermeer's paintings, a pitcher of wine is on the table. The birdcage at left on the back wall was apparently added by a later artist as a symbol of how the girl should behave and can be read as a warning to avoid the company of men who urge young women to drink.

Plate 13

WOMAN IN BLUE READING A LETTER

c.1662-1664; 18¼in x 15½in (46.5cm x 39cm); oil on canvas.
Rijksmuseum, Amsterdam

This could be a portrait of Vermeer's wife Catharina when she was well into one of her fifteen known pregnancies (eight of their children survived infancy). Whether it is her or not is only speculation, but the woman is reading a letter, a familiar Vermeer device, and she is shown with the left side of her face to the viewer, another typical Vermeer pose. Behind her is the same map of Holland Vermeer showed in *The Officer and the Laughing Girl*-by Balthasar van Berckenrode, it is dated to 1620. The atmosphere is of calm and quiet expectation-waiting for the baby and waiting for the returning husband. All of this is emphasized by the pale and muted coloring. Nothing jars and nothing dominates but the woman's face is the absolute focus of the painting, gently lit in profile by light falling from an unseen window.

Plate 14

THE MUSIC LESSON

c.1662-1665; 29in x 25½in (73.3cm x 64.5cm); oil on canvas.
The Royal Collection © Her Majesty Queen Elizabeth II

Here the figures almost serve the function of a still life composition at the background of the painting. The large blank walls and geometric black and white marble floor catch the eye before it is drawn to the black and white costume of the music teacher. The opulent Turkish rug in the right foreground is an indication of the burghers wealth and Dutch Far Eastern trading success. A hint of local trade is shown by the prominent white Delftware jug standing proud on the table at the edge of the picture. The girl's face is apparently hidden from our view, but glance up and her reflection lies in the mirror above her instrument (*a clavecin*). although the face in the mirror is pointing in a slightly different direction. On the clavecin is written an inscription *Musica Letitiae Comes Medicine Dolorum*, -"Music is the Companion of Joy, the Medicine of Sorrow." In the center of the painting lies an abandoned bass viol and it is possible that the couple have been playing a duet.

The painting partially seen on the right is a reproduction of *Roman Charity* by Dirck van Baburen. It was owned by Maria Thins, Vermeer's mother-in-law. *The Music Lesson* was bought by King George III when it was passed off to his buyer as being by the (at the time) much better considered Dutch painter Pieter de Hoogh. To establish this subterfuge a false signature was appended to the painting.

Plate 15

WOMAN WITH A LUTE

c.1664; 20¼in x 18in (51.4cm x 45.7cm); oil on canvas.
The Metropolitan Museum of Art, New York. Bequest of Collis P. Huntington, 1925

Vermeer again uses the composition of a darkened room with diffuse light coming in through a window on the left of the painting. Again the light falls predominantly on the young woman's face and upper dress. While tuning her lute her attention has been caught by something happening in the street outside, and she turns her head to peer through the window. Behind her on the wall is a large map of western Europe published by Jodicus Hondius in 1613. This copy is probably of the reprinted edition by Joan Blaeu in 1659. The painting is almost monochrome apart from the splash of golden yellow of the girl's ermine-trimmed bodice. Unfortunately much of the subtlety and detail of the painting has been lost through the passage of time and discoloration-a violin and sheets of music have been lost in the darkness of the floor.

Plate 16

WOMAN HOLDING A BALANCE

c.1664; 16¾in x 15in (42.5cm x 38cm); oil on canvas.
Widener Collection, © 1997 Board of Trustees, National Gallery of Art, Washington, D.C.

This painting is also called *Interior with a Lady Weighing Gold*. The subject is undoubtedly allegorical in meaning. The woman stands in darkness except for a chink of light creeping in around the curtain edge that bathes her face in radiance. The initial impression is that the painting is a study of a lady weighing her jewels-Amsterdam has long held a reputation as a world center for the jewelry trade, especially diamonds, In front of her lies an impressive selection of jewels, and she certainly looks content with her belongings. Partially seen behind her on the wall is a painting of the *Last Judgement* when souls are weighed for their worth. The painting is significant and Vermeer may be indicating that worldly wealth counts for nothing at St Peter's Gate. A mirror glints on the wall in front of the woman so she can watch her own reflection as she awaits her destiny. She looks calm and considering, content to let the balance decide for her. Upon close scrutiny it becomes clear that the scales she is holding are actually empty so she appears to be weighing her options-does she choose worldly wealth as shown by her jewels or the spiritual wealth of the Christian life?

Plate 17

WOMAN WITH A PEARL NECKLACE

c.1664; 21½in x 17¾in (55cm x 45cm); oil on canvas.
Staatliche Musecn zu Berlin, Preussischer Kulturbesitz, Gemäldcqalcric

This beautiful study of a sumptuously dressed young woman admiring herself and her pearls in the mirror is a painting masterclass. Vermeer uses his oil paints to perfection; the subject's furs and silks look as vibrant as any artist could achieve, and his use of light and space give the painting a unique tension and reality. She is ready to go out and socialize; her face, hair, and clothes are perfect and she looks completely satisfied with her presentation. The light and dark contrast strongly against each other with the predominant light illuminating the upper half of the painting and little obvious detail emerging in the darker portion of the room to distract attention from the woman. Pearls were significant for Vermeer as they signify purity, and there is little to suggest that this woman is anything other than she seems. Although this is one of Vermeer's most famous paintings, the earliest record of its provenance is from an obscure sale in the 1880s when it was bought for very little.

Plate 18

YOUNG WOMAN WITH A WATER PITCHER

c.1664-1665; 18in x 16in (45.7cm x 40.6cm); oil on canvas.
The Metropolitan Museum of Art, New York. Gift of Henry G. Marquand, 1889

This is an altogether lighter, brighter study of a woman opening the window to enjoy the sunshine and fresh air. Her figure is thrown into relief against the creamy-yellow wall, and her somewhat severe blue-black and gold costume is immaculate. The folds of her starched white headdress are detailed through the masterful execution of shadows. Vermeer's composition and use of space are exemplary and every aspect of the composition is in perfect balance with the other elements. The table in front of the young woman is covered with an elaborate Turkish rug and laid with a silver platter and jug. These are so highly polished that the rug is reflected on the underside of the plate. Also on the table is the young woman's jewel box, with blue ribbons spilling out. Draped over the chair in the background is a blue dress to match the ribbons-perhaps she is preparing her outfit for an important social occasion later that day. On the wall behind her hangs a map of Holland. The photographic detail of the painting shows an artist at the height of his powers, a superbly capable master of the medium.

Plate 19

GIRL WITH A PEARL EARRING

c.1665; 18¼in x 15¾in (46.5cm x 40cm); oil on canvas.
Mauriishuis, The Hague

This beautiful portrait is one of Vermeer's most famous and admired works. He uses his favorite yellows and blues set against a black background to accentuate the girl's beauty. It is actually a very simple composition: there is no elaboration of costume or fuss with hairstyle; instead, the girl's hair is completely hidden under twists of silk. Her face is framed by the dark background and highlighted by the white slash of her collar. The girl is turning to look over her shoulder and seems to be speaking to Vermeer. A huge single pearl hangs from her ear, half hidden in shadow-to own such a jewel her father or husband would have to be a wealthy man. Vermeer used the symbolism of pearls to illustrate purity. It has been suggested that this is Vermeer's daughter, but at the date of the painting his oldest girl, Maria, would only have been eleven and too young to be this sitter. Once again Vermeer's mastery of the techniques of putting oil on canvas do not hide the brilliance of his use of color, composition, and *chiaroscuro* to heighten atmosphere.

Plate 20

A LADY WRITING

c.1665-1670; 17¾in x 15¾in (45cm x 39.9cm); oil on canvas.
Gift of Harry Waldron Hauemeyer and Horace Haucmeycr, Jr., in memory of their father,
Horace Hauemeyer, © 1996 Board of Trustees, National Gallery of Art, Washington, D.C.

The young woman is looking straight at the viewer with a calm and mildly enquiring expression; she is in the process of writing a letter with a quill pen. The light in the room bathes her in a golden glow and singles her out from her darker surroundings. She is dressed in the familiar yellow silk and ermine-trimmed jacket already seen in *Woman with a Lute* and *Woman with a Pearl Necklace*, and used again in *Mistress and Maid*, *The Love Letter*, and *The Guitar Player*. She is wearing large single-drop pearl earrings and her hair is caught up in ribbons. Such an emphasis on pearls is so that the viewer is in no doubt about her purity and fidelity. A pearl necklace lies by her hand on the table. Another regular prop is the lion-headed chair that appears regularly in Vermeer's paintings. Behind her on the wall is a large dark painting.

Plate 21

THE CONCERT

c.1665-1666; 28½in x 25½in (72.5cm x 64.7cm); oil on canvas.
Isabella Steuiart Gardner Museum, Boston

For this painting Vermeer sets his easel further back from his subjects than usual to show a substantial portion of the room. The three people are calmly playing music either for their own pleasure or giving a musical performance for an unseen audience- Vermeer gives no hint as to which. The girl almost in the center of the composition is sitting at an elaborately painted harpsichord. In front of her and to the right of the picture her companion is singing from a sheet of paper and beating time with her hand. Between them, a seated man with his back to the viewer is playing a lute. The viewer's eye is drawn into the picture through the device of the black and white tiled floor. In the foreground a stringed instrument lies on the floor beside a table piled with a Turkish rug, violin, and music sheets. On the wall behind the musicians are two large paintings; on the left a second pastoral scene (the first is on the painted lid of the harpsichord) featuring a dead tree. However, the painting on the right is a reproduction of Dirck van Babureri's *Procuress*, a painting owned by Vermeer's mother-in-law. This Procuress now hangs in the Museum of Fine Arts in Boston. Vermeer must have particularly admired this work as he also included it in his painting *Lady Seated at a Virginal*. However, it contributes a note of ambiguity to the picture. Is Vermeer hinting at the availability of the young ladies for procurement? This painting disappeared over a decade ago when it was one of eleven stolen on March 18, 1990, from the Isabella Stuart Gardner Museum, Boston.

Plate 22

GIRL WITH THE RED HAT

c.1666-1667; 9in x 7in (23.2cm x 18.1cm); oil on canvas.
Andreu. W Mellon Collection, © 1996 Board of Trustees,
National Gallery of Art, Washington, D.C.

This is the only known Vermeer to be painted on a wood panel as opposed to his usual canvas. Also unusually for Vermeer, the girl is looking to her and our right. She is wearing a dramatic red fur-trimmed hat and appears to be chatting to Vermeer as he paints her portrait. Most of her face is in shadow and only the tip of her nose, chin, and left cheek are illuminated by light. She also wears a white high-necked ruffled shirt with a blue-figured jacket or cloak over the top. She is sitting sideways on one of Vermeer's signature lion-headed chair-as seen in so many of his paintings. The way Vermeer has spotted bright highlights onto the lion heads in the manner of an unfocussed camera is used as evidence of his use of a camera obscura. In common with previous sitters she is wearing large single-drop pearl earrings. The entire background of the painting is filled with what appears to be a tapestry hanging.

Plate 23

ALLEGORY OF PAINTING

c.1666-1667; 47¼in x 39½in (120cm x 100cm); oil on canvas.
Kunsthistorisches Museum, Vienna

This rich and complex painting, full of symbol and meaning, was entitled *De Schilderkonst* (The Art of Painting) by Vermeer's widow, and it is known by both these titles. The title *De Schilderkonst* is important, because this indicates that it is very unlikely that the artist depicted is Vermeer himself, something some authorities have suggested. Had it been Vermeer, Catharina would surely have ascribed the painting as being a self-portrait. The painting harks back to Vermeers early allegorical works. The artist is portrayed in historic Burgundian clothes: his model is posing as Clio-the muse of history-shown by the laurel wreath on her head, her book, and the trumpet of fame in her right hand. The book is identified as being the works of Thucydides, the classical Greek historian. The tapestry curtain falling across the left of the composition gives the impression that the viewer is watching the pair from another room, while the eye is skillfully drawn into the composition by the black and white floor tiles. On the back wall hangs a large map of the Netherlands produced by Nicolaes Visscher in 1592 when the country was still occupied by the Spanish. A crease runs down the map visually dividing the Dutch Republic from the Spanish occupied lands of Catholic Flanders. The brass chandelier bears the double-headed eagles of the Spanish House of Hapsburg so recently ejected from the United Provinces. The lack of candles in the sconces are presumed to show Vermeer's opinion of the fallen empire and their lack of power. On the table is what appears to be a death mask: scholars propose that it is of Willem of Orange and taken from his tomb in the Prinsenhof in Delft. This painting was in Vermeer's estate when he died, but as one of his more valuable assets its ownership became contested after his death. His mother-in-law did everything she could to keep this particular painting in the family, but it went into the auction sale of Vermeer's goods to payoff his creditors, in spite of her best endeavors.

Plate 24

PORTRAIT OF A YOUNG WOMAN

c.1666-1667; 72½in x 15¾in (44.5cm x 40cm); oil on canvas.
The Metropolitan Museum of Art, New York. Gift of Mr and Mrs Charles Wrightsman, in memory
of Theodore Rousseau, 1979

An earnest young woman half smiles at the viewer over her left shoulder in this simple, beautiful work. There is little color anywhere on the canvas. The young woman's surroundings are in complete darkness, and the light only shines on her face and the starched white shawl around her shoulder. The back of her head is defined by a darker white veil trailing down her back-without this device her face would be swimming in the dark without definable end. A discreet, yet elegant, pearl earring can just be seen. The feeling is of the purity and excellence of this young woman, little more than a girl really, at the threshold of adult life. It has been speculated that this girl is Maria, Vermeer's eldest daughter, but there is no evidence to confirm this.

Plate 25

MISTRESS AND MAID

c.1667-1668; 35½in x 31in (90.2cm x 78.7cm); oil on canvas.
The Frick Collection, New York

The two women depicted in this painting are in excited conversation about a letter that the maid is holding. But as she leans forward, is the maid taking the letter or offering it? Her mistress holds her hand to her chin as if uncertain what to do with the missive. But is she receiving it or sending it? The former appears the more likely, as she is caught in the act of writing a letter herself. Significantly, she is not reaching out to take the paper. Whether she is receiving or giving, she is in a quandry. The letter is undoubtedly one her family would not approve of and her maid must keep her correspondence a secret. The background is completely black, throwing both women into relief and concentrating attention on their faces and clothes. The mistress is wearing the now familiar yellow satin and ermine-trimmed jacket that fills the painting with color and vibrancy.

Plate 26

THE ASTRONOMER

1668; 20in x 17¾in (50cm x 45cm); oil on canvas.
Musée du Louvre, Paris

The Astronomer and *The Geographer* were probably painted as companion pieces; they are recorded as being together in 1713 and were sold as a pair in 1729. It is possible that this is a portrait of Antony van Leeuwenhoek, the Delft scientist and inventor of the microscope. He was an exact contemporary of Vermeer's and they undoubtedly knew each other as two important men of Delft. Leeuwenhoek was appointed by the city council to be Vermeer's executor for the tricky disposal of his goods and senlernent with his creditors after his death.

The seventeenth century was the great age of scientific discovery and it is no surprise that the subject matter of a scholar at work was a favorite with many contemporary Dutch artists. *The Astronomer* is looking at a celestial globe as if to check to make sure that the text in front of him is correct. The globe is known to be made by Jodocus Hondius in 1600. On the table beside his hand is a richly embroidered green and blue tapestry and an astrolabe, an instrument for measuring the altitudes of the stars. The painting on the wall behind is *The Finding of Moses* which symbolizes the new seventeenth century scientific discoveries, many of which were made by van Leeuwenhoek.

The composition and treatment of this painting are reminiscent of *Girl Reading a Letter at an Open Window* except for the use of greens rather than reds as the predominant contrast color. However, here Vermeer's mature technique is more subtle and the play of light on the fabrics gives a greater impression of texture and weight of fabric. This is only the second of two paintings that Vermeer dated; the other is the *Procuress*.

Plate 27

THE GEOGRAPHER

c.1668-1669; 21in x 18¼in (53cm x 46.6cm); oil on canvas.
Städelschcs Kunstinstitut, Frankfurt-am-Main, Germany

Compare this painting to *The Astronomer* and it is clear that they are similar in many respects and would have been painted as a pair. This time Vermeer presents a three-quarters view of his subject and bathes him and his surroundings in light. He looks as if he is in his dressing gown and has hurried to his charts to check out an idea that came to him during the night. He holds a pair of dividers in his right hand and he is absorbed in his work, as if calculating figures in his head, as he leans over a chart. Vermeer only made minor changes for the background of these two paintings: the composition of the roorn is the same with only details changed. The terrestrial globe is the twin of the celestial globe in *The Astronomer* and was also made by Jodocus Hondius in 1600. Behind the astronomer on the wall is an early seventeenth century map of Europe similar to a well-known chart by William Blaeu. The cupboard appears near identical to the one in *The Astronomer*, as does the window in all except the colored central stained glass. Otherwise many of the elements echo each other in treatment. The inscription on the wall was added in the nineteenth century but Vermeer himself signed this painting on the cupboard just above the geographer's head.

Plate 28

THE LOVE LETTER

c.1669-1670; 17½in x 15¼in (44cm x 38.5cm); oil on canvas.
Rijksmuseum, Amsterdam

In this exquisite painting, the viewer is looking through from a darkened room at two women lit up by the play of sunlight. Immediately, one is made to feel like a spy or voyeur. In fact, this painting is a mirror echo of *Allegory of Painting* in the way the curtain and door frame the figures and in the way the black and white tiled floor leads the eye into the center of the painting. The room is furnished more luxuriously than in his other paintings.

The sitting woman, the mistress of the house, has been interrupted from playing her either by the arrival of a love letter. She is looking anxiously at her maid as if questioning whether anyone saw her receive the missive. Her maid on the other hand looks amused at her mistress's trepidation. The idle broom and ignored laundry basket are significant indications that she has been playing music and dreaming of her lover rather than doing her housework. The paintings of open skies and windy weather on the wall behind indicate her longing to escape the confines of her house and run off with her lover. Vermeer's assurance of composition and the use of the familiar golden jacket-this time seen with its accompanying skirt-in such contrast to the sombre surroundings provide a real tour de force.

Plate 29

THE LACEMAKER

c.1669-1670; 9½in x 8¼in (24.5cm x 21cm); oil on canvas.
Musée du Louvre, Paris

This painting shows Vermeer's painstaking attention to detail. The lacemaker needs good light to be able to knot her lace without making mistakes and so both she and her work glow in yellowed light-tiny pinpoints of color sparkle across the painting to suggest sunlight. Delft was well known for lacemaking and Vermeer's wife may well have been proficient in the art. Vermeer certainly knows sufficient about the subject to render accurately the posture of the girl at her work, as well as the bobbins, pins, and threads. The background is a plain wall that throws into relief the girl and her work. As with so many of his works Vermeer dresses his subject in yellow and blues with only a tiny contrast of other bright color in the painting. The first record of *The lacemaker* shows that it belonged to a Delft bookseller, Jacob Dissius, in 1696. It then disappeared for a century and subsequently changed hands many times before being acquired by The Louvre in 1890.

Plate 30

LADY WRITING A LETTER WITH HER MAID

c.1670; 28in x 23in (71.1cm x 58.4cm); oil on canvas.
National Gallery of Ireland, Dublin

In this painting the mistress of the house is sitting at her table earnestly writing a letter while her maid idly looks out of the window while she waits for her mistress to finish. Perhaps, she posted as a lookout for her mistress's husband to warn her should he return to the house. Daylight fills the room and a gentle breeze is billowing the curtain. The mistress is a wealthy woman, as her dress and jewelry attest. This is confirmed by the tasteful room furnishings-a large oil painting on the wall, a rich Turkish rug on the table, and elegant fringing on the chair seat. On the floor in front of the lady lies a crumpled sheet of paper: a first attempt at a difficult letter, maybe. Her seal and sealing wax lie beside the paper as if they were all brushed off the table in frustration.

The oil painting behind the figures occupies almost a quarter of the scene. It is the same painting as shown in *The Astronomer*, although considerably larger in size. The painting is entitled *The Finding of Moses* and symbolizes for the viewer that someone must be rescued and looked after, but who that is not clear from the painting. The maid is looking through the same stained glass window at the emblem of temperance that Vermeer painted in two of his earlier works.

Plate 31

ALLEGORY OF FAITH

c.1671-1674; 45in x 35in (114.3cm x 88.9cm); oil on canvas.
The Metropolitan Museum of Art, New York.
Bequest of Michael Friedsman, 1931. The Friedsman Collection

With this work Vermeer returns to large-scale religious subjects; it may well have
been the result of a commission, possibly from the Delft Jesuit order. The composition
the heavy with Catholic symbolism. The woman is Eve, and she is half sitting
while leaning on an altar. One foot rests on a terrestrial globe and her right hand is
splayed over her heart in supplication. She is looking up at a suspended clear glass
globe, possibly a symbol of human reason. In front of her on the altar is an open
Bible, a standing crucifix, and a rich glass and gold chalice. The crucifix the given
predominance by the gilt leather panel behind it. On the typical Dutch black and white
flagged floor lies a serpent crushed under a large stone with blood pouring from its
mouth; nearby lies a fresh apple. The painting clearly shows the triumph of good over
evil. Eve is flanked on one side by a large draped tapestry curtain and behind her is
a large painting showing Christ on the cross. Here Vermeer has used some of his own
possessions as props for his painting. The ebony crucifix and the gilt leather panel
are both itemized in his effects after his death, as is the painting *Crucifixion* by Jacob
Jordaens.

Plate 32

THE GUITAR PLAYER

c.1672; 21in x 18¼in (53cm x 46.3cm); oil on canvas.
Kenwood, English Heritage as Trustees of the Iveagh Bequest, London

This painting is divided vertically by light-the left where the young musician sits is bright with light; the right where her table and book lie is much darker. All the action and interest in the painting is on the left-hand side, so the composition is deliberately one-sided. The elegantly dressed and coiffed young lady-in the now familiar yellow satin jacket is smiling and chatting as she plays on her beautiful guitar. Her face is half in light and half in shadow, and her necklace of pearls shines out around her throat. Behind her ringleted head is a brightly illuminated oil painting of a tree in an elaborate gold frame. Vermeer's brushwork is much freer than usual and some of his treatment of the fabric and the girl's hair is almost Impressionistic in execution. Vermeer still owned this painting when he died but his wife had to use it and another to settle an outstanding debt of 617 guilders with the master baker of Delft, Hendrick van Buyten. The painting eventually went to London and to its new home at Kenwood House from where it was stolen in 1974 by IRA supporters. Luckily it was recovered ten weeks later when it was found in a churchyard.

Plate 33

A YOUNG WOMAN STANDING AT A VIRGINAL

c.1673-1675; 20½in x 17½in (51.7cm x 45.2cm); oil on canvas.
Reproduced by Courtesy of the Trustees, National Gallery, London

One of Vermeer's last works, this painting is similar but not identical to *A Young Woman Seated at a Virginal*. It is thought by some to be an allegory of sacred love, as suggested by the painting of Cupid holding up a card in the background. Cupid has his love arrows ready, but the card indicates the chancy nature of falling in love-this is a reference to an entry in the popular book *Amorum Emblemata* (1608) by Otto van Veen who pleads for people to have only one lover. The young woman is standing sideways on but has turned her head to look at Vermeer. She conveys a curious stillness and aura of calm as she stands in her quietly elaborate laced and beribboned dress. Her hands are placed on an instrument called a virginal. Around the lower edge of the room are Delft tiles depicting peasants at work.

Plate 34

93

A YOUNG WOMAN SEATED AT A VIRGINAL

c.1673-1675; 20¼in x 18in (51.5cm x 45.5cm); oil on canvas.
Reproduced by Courtesy of the Trustees, National Gallery, London

This is a companion painting to *The Young Woman Standing at a Virginal* and Vermeer worked on both at the same time. This work is altogether darker although more elaborate and fuller with detail. In fact, the color palette is virtually the same. This time the young woman is sitting at her virginal playing music but she has turned to her left to look at the viewer. She is dressed in her full finery but her expression is noncommittal-as if she is disappointed to see the viewer entering the room rather than the person she is hoping for. The lid of her virginal sports a sunlit pastoral scene, but the large painting on the wall above and behind her is of Dirck van Baburen's *Procuress*, (now hanging in the Boston Museum of Fine Arts). The inclusion of this painting leads some critics to conclude that this painting is an allegory of profane love and that the young woman is not as pure as she would like us to think.

Plate 35

INDEX